This copy of

SING A NEW SONG

comes to

Mary-Jane ....

with love from

Sandra x 13·10·02 ....

Sing A New Song

British Library Cataloguing-in-Publication Data. A catalogue record for this book is available from the British Library

Published in the UK by Eagle, an imprint of Inter Publishing Service (IPS) Ltd, 59 Woodbridge Road, Guildford, Surrey GU1 4RF.

Typeset by The Electronic Book Factory Ltd, Fife.
Printed by L.E.G.O., Italy.

ISBN No: 0 86347 127 7

SING A NEW SONG

WELL LOVED HYMNS AND CHORUSES

eagle

Guildford, Surrey

Such love pure as the whitest snow

Such love, pure as the whitest snow;
Such love, weeps for the shame I know;
Such love, paying the debt I owe;
O Jesus, such love.

Such love, stilling my restlessness;
Such love, filling my emptiness;
Such love, showing me holiness;
O Jesus, such love.

Such love, springs from eternity;
Such love, streaming through history;
Such love, fountain of life to me;
O Jesus, such love.

Graham Kendrick

As the deer pants for the water

As the deer pants for the water,
So my soul longs after You.
You alone are my heart's desire
And I long to worship You.

> You alone are my strength, my shield,
> To You alone may my spirit yield.
> You alone are my heart's desire
> And I long to worship You.

I want You more than gold or silver,
Only You can satisfy.
You alone are the real joy-giver
And the apple of my eye.

You're my Friend and You are my Brother,
Even though you are a King.
I love You more than any other,
So much more than anything.

Martin Nystrom

Be Thou my vision

Be Thou my vision, O Lord of my heart;
Naught be all else to me, save that Thou art –
Thou my best thought, by day or by night,
Waking or sleeping, Thy presence my light.

Be Thou my Wisdom, Thou my true Word;
I ever with Thee, Thou with me, Lord;
Thou my great Father, I Thy true son;
Thou in me dwelling, and I with Thee one.

Riches I heed not, nor man's empty praise,
Thou mine inheritance, now and always.
Thou and Thou only, first in my heart,
High King of heaven, my treaure Thou art.

Ancient Irish tr by Mary Elizabeth Byrne
Versified by Eleanor Henrietta Hull

Great is Thy faithfulness

Great is Thy faithfulness, O God my Father,
There is no shadow of turning with Thee;
Thou changest not, Thy compassions they fail not,
As Thou hast been Thou forever wilt be.

Great is Thy faithfulness!
Great is Thy faithfulness!
Morning by morning new mercies I see;
All I have needed Thy hand hath provided,
Great is Thy faithfulness, Lord, unto me!

Summer and winter, and springtime and harvest,
Sun, moon and stars in their courses above,
Join with all nature in manifold witness
To Thy great faithfulness, mercy and love.

Pardon for sin and a peace that endureth,
Thine own dear presence to cheer and to guide;
Strength for today and bright hope for tomorrow,
Blessings all mine, with ten thousand beside!

T.O. Chisholm

I heard the voice of Jesus say

I heard the voice of Jesus say:
Come unto Me and rest;
Lay down, thou weary one, lay down
Thy head upon My breast!
I came to Jesus as I was,
Weary, and worn, and sad;
I found in Him a resting place,
And He has made me glad.

I heard the voice of Jesus say;
Behold, I freely give
The living water; thirsty one,
Stoop down and drink, and live!
I came to Jesus and I drank
Of that life-giving stream;
My thirst was quenched, my soul revived,
And now I live in Him.

Horatius Bonar

I trust in thee, O Lord

I trust in thee, O Lord
I say, "Thou art my God".
My times are in thy hand
My times are in thy hand.
Blessed be the Lord,
For he has wondrously shown
his steadfast love to me,
his steadfast love to me.

M Warrington

P. Mönsted. 1897.

Like a river glorious

Like a river glorious is God's perfect peace,
Over all victorious, in its bright increase.
Perfect, yet it floweth fuller every day;
Perfect, yet it groweth deeper all the way.

Stayed upon Jehovah, hearts are fully blest;
Finding, as He promised, perfect peace and rest.

Hidden in the hollow of His blessed hand,
Never foe can follow, never traitor stand;
Not a surge of worry, not a shade of care,
Not a blast of hurry touch the Spirit there.

Frances R Havergal

Thy hand O God has guided

Thy hand, O God, has guided
   Thy flock from age to age;
The wondrous tale is written,
   Full clear, on every page;
Our fathers owned Thy goodness,
   And we their deeds record;
And both of this bear witness,
   One Church, one Faith, one Lord.

Thy mercy will not fail us,
   Nor leave Thy work undone;
With Thy right hand to help us,
   The victory shall be won;
And then, by men and angels,
   Thy name shall be adored,
And this shall be their anthem,
   One Church, one Faith, one Lord.

E H Plumptre (1821–91)

Will your anchor hold in the storms of life?

Will your anchor hold in the storms of life,
When the clouds unfold their wings of strife?
When the strong tides lift, and the cables strain,
Will your anchor drift, or firm remain?

We have an anchor that keeps the soul
Steadfast and sure while the billows roll;
Fastened to the rock which cannot move,
Grounded firm and deep in the Saviour's love!

Will your anchor hold in the straits of fear?
When the breakers roar and the reef is near;
While the surges rave, and the wild winds blow,
Shall the angry waves then your bark o'erflow?

Will your anchor hold in the floods of death,
When the waters cold chill your latest breath?
On the rising tide you can never fail,
While your anchor holds within the veil.

Priscilla Jane Owens (1829–99)

Abide with me

Abide with me; fast falls the eventide;
The darkness deepens; Lord, with me abide
When other helpers fail, and comforts flee,
Help of the helpless, O abide with me.

Swift to its close ebbs out life's little day;
Earth's joys grow dim, its glories pass away;
Change and decay in all around I see:
O Thou who changest not, abide with me!

I need Thy presence every passing hour;
What but Thy grace can foil the tempter's power?
Who like Thyself my guide and stay can be?
Through cloud and sunshine, O abide with me.

Henry Francis Lyte (1793–1847)

O love that wilt not let me go

O love that wilt not let me go,
I rest my weary soul in thee:
I give thee back the life I owe,
That in thine ocean depths its flow
May richer, fuller be.

O light that followest all my way,
I yield my flickering torch to thee:
My heart restores its borrowed ray,
That in thy sunshine's blaze its day
May brighter, fairer be.

O joy that seekest me through pain,
I cannot close my heart to thee:
I trace the rainbow through the rain,
And feel the promise is not vain,
That morn shall tearless be.

George Matheson

How precious O Lord is your unfailing love

How precious O Lord,
Is your unfailing love,
We find refuge in the shadow of Your wings.
We feast, Lord Jesus, on the abundance of Your house
And drink from Your river of delights.
With You is the fountain of life,
In Your light we see light,
With You is the fountain of life,
In Your light we see light.

Phil Rogers

In Heavenly Love Abiding

In heavenly love abiding,
No change my heart shall fear;
And safe is such confiding,
For nothing changes here:
The storm may roar without me,
My heart may low be laid;
But God is round about me,
And can I be dismayed?

Green pastures are before me,
Which yet I have not seen;
Bright skies will soon be o'er me,
Where darkest clouds have been;
My hope I cannot measure,
My path to life is free;
My Saviour has my treasure,
And He will walk with me.

Anna L Waring

You are my hiding place

You are my hiding place,
You always fill my heart with songs of deliverance,
Whenever I am afraid
I will trust in You,
I will trust in You;
Let the weak say I am strong
In the strength of my God.

Michael Leadner

G. Sheridan Knowles

Photographic credits

Eagle Publishing is grateful to The Fine Art Photographic Library (unless otherwise stated), the copyright holders of the reproduction rights, for their kind permission to reproduce the paintings selected.

Cover — Mackay, Thomas W, (1840–1916); *At the brook* (courtesy John Spink Fine Watercolours, London, © Bridgemen Art Library)

Page 5 — Abels, Jacobus Theodorus (1803–1866); *A winter landscape* (courtesy Owen Edgar)

Page 7 — Banks, William (1877–?); *Deer crossing a burn*

Page 8 — Rigolot, Albert Gabriel (1862–1932); *A summer's day on the river* (courtesy Anthony Mitchell Fine Paintings, Nottingham)

Page 11 — Strachan, Arthur Claude (1865–1954); *A beautiful herbacious border* (courtesy Haynes Fine Art, Broadway, Worcs.)

Page 13 — Mackay, Thomas W, (1840–1916); *At the brook* (© Bridgeman Art Library)

Page 15 — Darien, Henri-Gaston (1864–1926); *Une chaumière et un coeur* (courtesy Galerie Berko)

Page 16 — Monsted, Peder Monk (1859–1941); *A shady stream* (courtesy Burlington Paintings, London W1)

Page 19 — Shalders, George (1825–1873); *A shepherd boy and flock of sheep* (© Bridgeman Art Library, courtesy Christopher Wood Gallery, London)

Page 21 — James, David (active 1883–1897); *The flowing tide* (private collection)

Page 23 — Cole, Reginald Rex Vicat (1870–1940); *September leaves* (courtesy Nick Drummond)

Page 25 — Lundby, Anders Andersen (1840–1923); *The woods in silver and gold* (courtesy Polak Gallery, London SW1)

Page 27 — Monsted, Peder Monk (1859–1941); *The lake in the woods* (courtesy Burlington Paintings, London W1)

Page 29 — Mitchell, C L (circa 1900); *A day at the river* (courtesy Anthony Mitchell Fine Paintings, Nottingham)

Page 31 — Knowles, George Sheridan (1863–1931); *The rose arch* (courtesy Walker Gallery, Harrogate)